Poetic Tourings

Luke Mayo

Presentation by *BookLeaf Publishing*

Web: www.bookleafpub.com

E-mail: info@bookleafpub.com

ISBN: 9789358316438

First edition 2023

This book is dedicated to its readers. I hope you find a way to explore the world, be inspired by it and contribute something positive to it.

ACKNOWLEDGEMENT

There are a great many people in my life who have contributed positively to my travels, my poetry and my life. I aim to thank them here.

The places I've worked and volunteered, who have enabled me to financially afford to make the journeys I've made. In their own way, my workplaces have had their own hand in helping me to develop my poetry. For that, I'm grateful.

The University of Suffolk, and specifically its English Department, has enabled me to find, develop and pursue my creative voice. I will always love the staff and classmates I've met who have helped me on my way.

Finally, my lovely family. I have accompanied them on many journeys, and those journeys were enriched by our shared presence and experiences. I thank my family for being with me and supporting me through the journey of life.

I love you all.

PREFACE

It strikes me that there are two kinds of people: those who reckon the world is tiny and insignificant in the big, wide context of the cosmos, and those who think our planet is actually quite special, wondrous and inspiring.

I'm the second one.

I've not seen a lot of what this world has to offer, but the things I have seen are incredible. Different places in Europe and America have impressed me with their sights, sounds and people. Even my native England has some rather cool things going on.

When it comes to processing and channelling my experiences creatively, poetry is my chosen method. Hence the existence of this book, which contains writings inspired by my travels. I hope you enjoy reading it.

A Stable Place to Be

The person who roams the world
The person who yearns for adventure
The person who travels to all
The person who aspires to all destinations

I am not this person

I am the home lover
The comfort creature
The former of small habits
The content in one place
The spirit of the status quo

However
And it's a big however
My attachment to the status quo
It's not permanent or omnipresent
It can be departed from

Flights of fancy can be fun

Seeing new things
Exploring new places
Meeting new people
They help me appreciate the normal

Deviations from the norm
Rebellion from the same old thing

They enrich the status quo
That's why they're precious

Travelling Dynamics

To make your journey
It costs money
It costs time
It costs your soul

Prodded and probed by security
What are you hiding?
The dissection of luggage
Can you carry it on?

Can you carry on?

If the destination is worth going
Carrying on the carry-on is worth doing

Rail, road, sea, sky
All routes to get by
Across language barriers and time zones
Good luck sleeping in a rickety seat
Other peoples' noises
Other peoples' farts

Then you arrive
The journey is soon forgotten
The place you were going is here

Replace the bad memories with good ones

Navigating the dynamics of travel
A game worth playing

Cultures of Different Kinds

All of us humans
Members of our race
We are all the same
Because we are all different

The way we speak
Our way of doing things
Our tenets of belief

As many and as variant as us all

The further you go
The more differences you see
Go to the horizon
And the horizon goes further away

Get to know your fellow humans
Get ready for expansion
Edges of reality
They are ours to affect

Our differences
Do they separate us?
Do they connect us?

That's our choice

We meet each other
Get to know each other
See how many paths there are

The cultures of different kinds
Bringing awe and wonder to our minds

Chasing the Rainbow's End

Treading the path of life
Sun shines behind me
Dark clouds brew before me

Fear and trepidation rise within me

Down comes the rain
Washing away my life
My soul
My joy

I long to end the journey now

Then something bright snatches my eye
A collection of colours
An arched frame for the road ahead

The rainbow is here

The journey doesn't seem pointless now
The rainbow lights the way

Some day
Somehow
I'll reach the journey's end

Bonny Bo'ness

Those of us who love nature
Who yearn for its presence
Who love its touch
Who crave its breath of life
Who appreciate its beauty

There's a place we can have it all
Its name is Bo'ness

The District of Lakes
Rolling, running green-scapes
Mountains connecting land to sky
Water and plants to sustain life's beauty

Bo'ness brings the bounty

Come express your creativity
Come be inspired by art
Come do good things

The critical thinkers
The practical doers
The leaders of bright futures
The visionaries of wonder
You are welcome here

Bo'ness
Where heroes are born and bred

9

A Place Called York

Respect for history
Love of mystery
A cultured world
Layers unfurled

It's all in York

Emanating from the walls
Clamouring from the buildings
Sounding softly on the breeze
Tales from previous days, years and centuries

The Vikings did their thing
They lived their lives
How little they knew
York would preserve their legacy

What if our legacy is also preserved?

The journey never ends
The exploring never stops
The search for the past
It leads to the future

I love York's stories

I love York's sights
I love York's people
I love York

Keeping Up With Krakow

The joys of Poland
The horrors of Auschwitz
The wonders of the salt mines
The blessings of good people

Find it all in Krakow

The beatific inspiration of parks and buildings
The nightmare of prison camps where life was
slaughtered
Laughs and screams echoing as memories

Both are found in Krakow
Both remind us of human nature
Best and worst in extremes
Heroes and villains thrust together

We hear the stories
We learn from them
We carry them forward
We aspire for better
All thanks to Krakow

Krakow is the custodian of humanity's tales

When in Rome

Roam from home
Roam to Rome
See history
Do culture
Meet destiny

The arena of sporting extremities
Man versus beast
Art of canvas and stone
Communities of faith and acceptance

Rome homes it all

A place where humanity sees its achievements
Where the path leads humanity on
Where creativity spawns creativity
Where art feeds on itself

Inspiration to do something good
Encouragement to live your best life
It's here before your eyes

When in Rome
You're at home

No Menace in Venice

A world on water
Travel the streets by boat
Main streets and back streets
Character expands to fill both

Mammal, fish and bird
Come together as one
Ghettos and gondolas
Buildings and boats

Venice is where they are

The embodiment of Italy
The spirit of humanity
The town of welcome
The habitat of happy

A world on its own
Sustained by its people
Journey of a community

A Venetian world of wonder

Stories from the Strip

A world where currency is king
A world where all wares are pedalled
A world where the gawdy is applauded

Welcome to the Las Vegas Strip

Massive lights and sounds
Seediness seeping from every pore
Money is the sole goal
All methods welcome

Sex
Drugs
Rock
Roll
Except not the last two

The magic is a firework
A bright bang disappears into smoke
Rock and roll?
Rank and no soul

Genuine talent
Positive fun
Found if you look hard enough

Sadly few and far between

Tawdriness
Thy name is Vegas
Spirits from the shallows salute you

Big Memories of the Big Apple

The iconic statue of freedom and womanhood
The dizzying heights of Empire State
The woosh and spray of Niagra Falls
The bright, buzzing commerce of Times Square

I've been the tourist
I've seen them all

A city of sights
A city of humans
A city of stories
A city of adventures

Hours and miles of travel
Clocked up on the streets of NYC

I went to the Big Apple
I returned with big memories
Happy memories
Warm memories
Crazy memories

I will take them with me gladly

Characters of Charity

Dire straits
Lives on streets
Narcotic lifestyles
The onset of old age

One thing they have in common
The reliance on charity

Voices to guide
Hands to hold
Roads to walk

Half the population needs it
The other half does it

Registered charities
Staff and volunteers
Stalwart souls of support
Helping souls of desperation

I've met both souls
I've been both souls

Characters of charity
Bless them all

Confronting Phobias

Vast crowds of strangers
Are they watching me?
Are they judging me?
Are they dangerous?
Am I dangerous?

Places set high in the sky
One look down swoops my soul
Though my body stands still
My brain takes me to bad places
An unstable reality of imagination

Darkened rooms of unknown places
Breeding grounds of unfamiliarity
What's here?
What's not here?
What might be here?

Mistakes and failures
Lifelong marks on my soul
Overriding my successes
Dominating my existence
Never allowed to move on

See these fears

Confront them
Name them
Face them
They can be overcome

Phobias may be with us
Courage defines us

Enshrined for the Future

The forebears
The trailblazers
The innovators

Their deeds swayed history
Their marks changed the landscape
Their efforts improved their communities
Their statues will stand forever

Or so it was hoped

Those statues
Built with respect
Forged with heroism
Carved with admiration
Left to inspire those to come

But those to come didn't like it

Paint was flung
Graffiti was sprayed
Rude words were left
Statues reduced to rubble

Because they disagreed

Because they were offended
Because they couldn't imagine the differences
Because they couldn't tolerate their own
insecurities

What once were shrines
Now are landfill
Because people hate their history

Farewell to the Funny People

Their humour made us laugh
Their deaths made us cry
Their fighting spirits made us want to continue

Their compassion warmed our hearts
Their demons broke our hearts
Their love gave our hearts something to hang on
to

Their friendship gave us something to live for
Their passing reminds us that life is frail
Their achievements remind us that life is worth
living

They were here
They are gone
The same for us all

We bid farewell
And in their name
And in their honour
We aspire to a good life
Just like they did

Humiliation Highlights

A flurry of purchase orders
New hoover needed urgently
Cheapest option selected and sent for
Turns out it's a child's toy
Maximum humiliation follows

Season of mock exams
Essays on book characters
Glad that I studied and revised
Tell us about this character
I happily oblige
Turns out I misread the question
Wrong character written about
No marks received

Printing out a name tag
Professional identification
Four little letters for my name
Shouldn't be too hard
Shame about the mistype
Looks like I can't spell my own name

Water bottle in my bag
Intended for drinking
Becomes an explosion

My items ruined
My handwritten notes destroyed

Situations like this
Strung together in a scrapbook of cringe
Welcome to my life

Man's Best Friend

They sit beside us
They walk alongside us
They take their cues from us
They share our burdens with us

These loyal companions
These messengers from heaven
These personifiers of love

They are dogs

Our joys
Our woes
Our loneliness
Our torments
Our successes

Our dogs are there
By their human's side
Forever and for always
A friendship that never fails

The doghouse is a good place to be
A dog's life is a good one to live

Souls of the Library

Shelves upon shelves
Row after row
Conglomerations of books
Stories sewn together as one

These are the places I've worked

People pour their souls into their writing
Other people read those words
Inspiration sparks like a flame

I am the conduit
The interface
The library worker
Enabling the transactions
Coordinating the interactions

The passing of texts
The power of literature
Love spreading like a fiery passion
This is what I live for

I am one of the souls of the library

The Souls Who Serve

A common foe
A unifying enemy
A widespread destruction
This is what brings the natural order together

Evil which threatens the fabric of society
Those of us who watch have a choice
Fight or die
Freedom or falling

Find your allies
Come together
Every creature
Humans and animals
Side by side

Evil may threaten us
Our own goodness unites us
Division need not ensnare us

Humanity
The Animal Kingdom
Joined in liberation
Brave and hopeful
Not to be deterred

They all do their bit
Pigeons taking messages
Horses ferrying soldiers
Dogs sniffing suspicion
Humans expressing gratitude

They are the souls who serve
Heroes every one

www.ingramcontent.com/pod-product-compliance
Lightning Source LLC
La Vergne TN
LVHW051244200726
843510LV00011B/1677